More to explore

On some of the pages in this book, you will find coloured buttons with symbols on them. There are four different colours, and each belongs to a different topic. Choose a topic, follow its coloured buttons through the book, and you'll make some interesting discoveries of your own.

For example, on page 11 you'll find a blue button, like this, next to a big tortoise. The blue buttons are about record breakers.

Page 23

Record breakers

There is a page number in the button. Turn to that page (page 23) to find a blue button next to another record-breaking reptile. Follow all the steps through the book, and at the end of your journey you'll find out how the steps are linked, and discover even more information about this topic.

Evolution

Habitats

Plants

The other topics in this book are evolution, habitats and plants. Follow the steps and see what you can discover!

What are reptiles?

Reptiles are a group of animals that include crocodiles, tortoises, lizards and snakes. There are about 6,500 different reptiles in all, from the tiny thread snake that's no bigger than a worm to the massive Nile crocodile.

green water dragon

Many reptiles have scaly skins.

These smooth, overlapping scales belong to a snake.

The green water dragon has a tough, scaly skin that stops its body losing water. Some reptiles, such as tortoises, have horny plates instead of scales.

Reptiles

Claire Llewellyn

KINGFISHER

KINGFISHER

First published 2011 by Kingfisher
an imprint of Macmillan Children's Books
a division of Macmillan Publishers Limited
20 New Wharf Road, London N1 9RR
Basingstoke and Oxford
Associated companies throughout the world
www.panmacmillan.com

Illustrations by: Peter Bull Art Studio

ISBN 978-0-7534-3035-4

Copyright © Macmillan Children's Books 2011

1 3 5 7 9 8 6 4 2

1TR/1210/WKT/UNTD/140MA

A CIP catalogue record for this book is available from the British Library.

Printed in China

Picture credits

The Publisher would like to thank the following for permission to reproduce their material.
(t = top, b = bottom, c = centre, l = left, r = right):
Pages 4l Nature Picture Library/Mary McDonald; 4r Frank Lane Picture Agency (FLPA)/Chris Mattison; 5tl Photolibrary/Imagebroker; 5tr Nature/Tony Phelps; 5crt Shutterstock/fzd.it; 5crb Shutterstock/Dick Stada; 5bl Seapics; 5br Shutterstock/melissaf84; 6tl Photolibrary/Peter Arnold Images; 8t Photolibrary/Corbis; 8bl Photolibrary/Peter Arnold Images; 8br Photoshot/Anthony Bannister/NHPA; 9t FLPA/Piotr Naskrecki/Minden; 9bl Ardea/Francois Gohier; 9br Nature/Tim Macmillan/John Downer Productions; 10tl Photolibrary/Fotosearch Value; 12cl Nature/Anup Shah; 12cr Photolibrary/Animals Animals; 12b Photoshot/Anthony Bannister/NHPA; 13tl Photoshot/Andrea Bonetti/NHPA; 13tr Photolibrary/Jason Heller; 13cr Photoshot/A.N.T./NHPA; 13bl Photolibrary/Peter Arnold Images; 14tl Shutterstock/fivespots; 16c Ardea/Tomas Marent; 16b–17b FLPA/Sott Linstead/Minden; 17tl Photolibrary/Peter Arnold Images; 17cr Photolibrary/John Warburton-Lee; 17cl Photolibrary/White; 18bl Alamy/Anna Yu; 20cl FLPA/Larry West; 20cr Shutterstock/shao weiwei; 20b–21b Nature/Nature Production; 21tl FLPA/Michael & Patricia Fogden/Minden; 21tr & 21 br FLPA/Tomas Marent/Minden; 21cl Photolibrary/Peter Arnold Images; 22bl Nature/Anup Shah; 24l Photolibrary/Peter Arnold Images; 24r Photolibrary/OSF; 25tl Photolibrary/Martin Chillmaid; 25cr & 25br Photoshot/Anthony Bannister/NHPA; 25cl FLPA/Mitsuaki Iwago/Minden; 26bl Shutterstock/Mike Brake; 28l Corbis/Martyn Goddard; 28r Shutterstock/Roger Rosentreter; 28b Photoshot/Bob Gibbons/Woodfall; 29t FLPA/Claus Meyer/Minden; 29cl Photolibrary/All Canada Photos; 29cr Photolibrary/OSF; 29b Photolibrary/Image Source; 30tl Photoshot/Daniel Heuclin/NHPA; 30tr Photoshot/Ken Griffiths/NHPA; 30cr Photolibrary/Ingo Schilz/Imagebroker; 30bl Photolibrary/Design Pics Inc; 30br Corbis/Ron Dahlquist; 31clt Alamy/Michael Patrick O'Neill; 31clb Shutterstock/Maksymilian Skolik; 31br Shutterstock/Martin Horsky.

Contents

A baby tortoise
struggles out of
its leathery egg.

harlequin
snake

Hermann's
tortoise

Nile
crocodile

A gecko
is a type
of lizard.

Most baby reptiles hatch
from eggs. The eggs are
round or oval-shaped, and
are always laid on dry land.

leopard gecko

There are four **main
reptile groups**: the snakes,
the crocodilians (crocodiles and
alligators), the tortoises and
turtles, and the lizards.

green sea turtle

Sea turtles
have flippers
instead of feet
to help them
swim in the sea.

Page 23

What is this?

1   A sand snake hunts for lizards.

2   The colourful gila monster is poisonous.

3   A horned lizard basks in the evening sunshine.

A place to live

Reptiles are cold-blooded, which means their body temperature changes with their surroundings. They like warm places and some even live in the hot, harsh desert. Snakes slither beneath the sand, lizards hide in shady cracks and tortoises shelter in cool burrows.

It is dusk in the desert. The animals that hid from the hot sunshine during the day come out to look for food. The rattlesnake is a hunter, and wriggles over the warm sand to attack a desert rat. It also preys on lizards, small birds and baby jackrabbits. Lizards feed on ants and other insects or, like the desert tortoise, chew tough desert plants.

Page 15

4

5

6

This is a gila woodpecker peering out of the nest hole it has made in a cactus.

Reptile habitats

Reptiles live in rivers, oceans, forests, hills and even under the ground. To help them survive in their chosen habitat, many species have developed special body features or different ways of life.

Alligators live in fresh water. Their armoured bodies are waterproof. Flaps of skin seal their ears, nose and throat, and a double pair of eyelids protects their eyes.

The shingleback skink is a four-legged lizard that burrows in the ground. To better suit a life underground, some skinks have lost their legs and wriggle along like snakes.

A web-footed gecko peeks out of its desert burrow.

Webbed feet help to support the gecko on the fine, dry sand.

an alligator swimming under the water

Green skin with white markings helps to hide the snake in the dappled forest light.

The slinky **emerald tree boa** lives in the rainforests of South America. This expert climber rests by day, coiled up on the branch of a tree.

emerald tree boa

Wakey wakey! Garter snakes leave their hibernation chambers in spring.

This small **flying lizard** lives in the rainforests of Southeast Asia. It glides around its forest habitat, using the broad flaps of skin on the sides of its body as wings.

Draco lizard

Garter snakes live as far north as Canada. The climate is so cool here that the snakes have to hibernate for eight months of the year.

Page 26

What is this?

1. A marine iguana warms up on the rocks.

2. A young iguana is about to dive in.

3. A cactus finch looks for insects on a prickly pear.

Feeding time

Reptiles will eat all kinds of food. Most of them feed on other animals. Some lick up tiny insects, some hunt fish, birds or mice, and some kill even larger prey, such as pigs and deer. Other reptiles are vegetarian and feed on a variety of plants.

3

Page 30

Animals on the Galápagos Islands in the Pacific Ocean find food on land and under the sea. Marine iguanas dive into the water to nibble seaweed from the slimy rocks. Green turtles feed on seaweed, too, but also snap up jellyfish, shrimps and crabs. On shore, giant tortoises browse on cacti, grasses, fruits and vines.

4

Page 23

5

6

This is a green turtle's head. The turtle has a sharp, horny beak.

Finding a meal

Plodding plant-eaters, stealthy hunters or expert fishermen – whatever their diet, all reptiles have the perfect jaws to grab a meal and chew their food. Plant-eaters graze all day long, while some hunters can go for weeks without eating.

Peg-like teeth grasp the wriggly, slippery fish.

An Indian gharial snaps up a fish in its long, slender jaws. This freshwater hunter is one of the smaller members of the crocodile family.

Loggerheads and other sea turtles have beaky mouths.

The turtle crunches through crab, clam and conch shells.

egg-eating snake

An African egg-eating snake eats nothing but birds' eggs. It can swallow an egg much bigger than its head because its jaws, neck and body stretch like elastic.

A speckled **Tokay gecko** lunches on a leaf cricket. These insect-eaters live in rainforests but also enter people's homes. They scuttle upside down on ceilings, searching for their prey.

Tokay gecko

Tiny, clinging hairs under each toe help the gecko hold on.

small, sharp teeth for grasping creepy-crawly prey

bearded dragon

Tortoises and turtles have no teeth but they can still bite. Their hard, horny jaws have a very sharp edge.

Most snakes have sharp, backward-pointing teeth. The teeth help the snake to grasp its food and haul it down its throat.

python

Lizards have a wide variety of diets, so they have different kinds of teeth. Their teeth may be small and pointed, cone-shaped or jagged.

What is this?

① A chameleon zaps its insect prey.

② A wood mouse scampers over the forest floor.

③ The gaboon viper slides through the dry leaves.

①

Page 30

Stealthy hunters

Meat-eating reptiles must hunt for their food.
Most of them choose to ambush their prey.
They hide themselves among branches and
leaves, and keep very still. Sooner or later,
an animal passes and the hunter strikes.

Page 22

Page 30

In the shade of an African rainforest, reptiles are hunting for food. A gaboon viper has spotted a wood mouse and is about to attack it with its fangs. Nearby, a rock python wraps its coils around a monkey, squeezing it tighter and tighter. Meanwhile, a chameleon spies a passing insect and shoots out its long, sticky tongue to catch it.

This is a chameleon's eye. Each eye can swivel around separately to look for food.

Making a kill

Snakes and other reptile hunters have all the tools they need to make a kill. They have great camouflage to hide themselves, super-sharp senses to detect prey, and deadly weapons. Some snakes, for example, are armed with venom (poison).

Pit can detect body heat of nearby prey.

The eyelash pit viper hunts in the dark. Two deep pits on its head can sense the heat of animals nearby, and provide the viper with a target to attack.

veiled chameleon

A sedge viper's fangs spring forward as it opens its mouth.

Venom pumps out through the hollow fangs.

An African python does not kill with venom. Instead it coils itself tightly around its prey until it can no longer breathe. Snakes that hunt this way are called constrictors. This python has caught an unlucky gazelle.

A spitting cobra sprays venom to keep enemies away.

An unsuspecting cricket sits on a leaf.

A veiled chameleon spots a cricket. The eyes focus to judge the distance. Then the tongue shoots out and catches the insect.

Staying alive

Many animals hunt reptiles – but reptiles have clever ways to avoid being caught. Some of them confuse or surprise their attacker. Others make themselves look big and scary or are just too prickly to eat!

Page 14

What is this?

1 shingleback skink

2 A frilled lizard gapes and hisses loudly.

3 An eagle hunts for food for its chicks

? This is a shingleback skink's tail. It's the same shape as its head, so it confuses predators.

③

Reptiles face danger in the dry Australian Outback. A frilled lizard raises the ruff around its neck to scare away a wedge-tailed eagle. Nearby, a blue-tongued skink flashes its tongue to startle a prowling dingo. The thorny devil has a different defence. Its body is covered with hard spines that make it scratchy to eat.

Page 30

④

⑥

⑤

④ A blue-tongued skink sticks out its tongue at a dingo.

⑤ a thorny devil looking for ants

⑥ a mulgara on the hunt for lizards

How to survive

Reptiles live in a dangerous world and many of them have amazing defences to protect themselves from attack. Some reptiles use camouflage to hide. Others fool or confuse their attacker with a clever trick.

A chuckwalla wedges itself in a rocky crack.

The lizard fits so tightly that it cannot be caught.

The tortoise lives inside a strong shell. At the first sign of danger, it tucks in its head and hides inside its armoured home.

Tail will grow back in a few months.

The Japanese five-lined skink has a surprising trick for when it senses danger. It distracts its attacker by breaking off its tail and then runs for its life. The tail will carry on wriggling for as long as five minutes.

The milk snake pretends to be poisonous.

leaf-tailed
gecko

*Colours are the
same as a deadly
coral snake's.*

The leaf-tailed gecko
is perfectly hidden from
predators. This one has the
same colour and shape as
a leaf on the forest floor.

This leaf-tailed gecko
rests all day on the trunk
of a tree. Its colour and
pattern help it blend in
with the lichens that
grow on the bark.

The eastern hognose snake plays a
good trick on any would-be attacker.
It rolls on its back, sticks out its
tongue and pretends to be dead.
Most predators avoid dead meat,
so this play-acting may save its life.

five-lined
skink

A good mother

Most reptiles lay eggs in a nest, a hollow log or a hole in the ground. Usually, the females abandon their eggs but female crocodiles stay close by. They guard and care for their young until they can look after themselves.

Page 11

What is this?

1. broken eggshells left behind by young
2. nest mound of twigs, built away from the water
3. baby crocodile, or hatchling

? This is a young crocodile hatching out of its egg.

Page 26

4

5

6

Page 27

In a mangrove swamp in India, saltwater crocodiles have laid their eggs in nests made of rotting leaves, twigs and mud. Now, after nearly three months, the eggs are beginning to hatch. One mother helps to free the baby crocodiles by gently breaking open her nest. Then she scoops each one in her jaws and carries it to the water.

4 mangrove swamp

5 The mother carries her young to a safe pool .

6 A wild dog hopes to steal some eggs.

Young reptiles

Most reptiles hatch out of eggs with no parents to help them. The young face a dangerous world and must find food and try to survive. A few lizards and snakes do not hatch out of eggs. They are born live.

A young chameleon perches on its parent's horn.

A female green python warms her eggs by twitching her muscles.

Young pythons will turn green after six to eight months.

The Jackson's chameleon lives in such cool places that it doesn't lay its eggs in the chilly ground. Instead, the eggs stay warm inside the mother's body and she gives birth to live young.

Corn snakes hatch from eggs that are laid in leaf litter or an old log. The snakelings have a tiny spike on their snout to split the papery eggshell. They stay in the egg for a day or two, then slither away.

orn snake

A common tiger snake sheds its old skin.

The skin slips off like a sock.

leatherback turtle

As a **gecko** grows, its skin gets too tight. The pale, top layer of scales splits at the snout and peels away. Underneath there is a new, shiny skin in a larger size.

velvet gecko

eatherback turtles
y their eggs in
est holes on tropical
eaches. As soon as
ne young hatch, they
ace to the water. They feed
n tiny plants and animals
nat float in the sea.

Protecting reptiles

Many reptiles are in danger from humans. For example, turtles are hunted for their eggs, meat and shells, and poisoned by pollution. They also drown in fishing nets and are killed by high-speed boats. Turtles and other reptiles need protecting.

Page 18

Page 19

What is this?

1 green iguanas in a coconut palm tree

2 Females come ashore to lay their eggs at night.

3 A volunteer checks turtle's satellite ta

? This is a cruise ship. Visiting tourists can spoil the beaches where turtles like to breed.

It is the breeding season for leatherback turtles. On a beach in Costa Rica, the mothers are laying their eggs. Scientists and helpers work by moonlight, fitting electronic tags to the turtles so they can be tracked by satellite. The scientists also collect the eggs and take them to a hatchery. There, they will be safe from predators and people who dig them up to sell.

Page 15

4 Volunteers count and transport the eggs.

5 Turtles dig their nests high up the beach.

6 Wild dogs may steal and eat turtle eggs.

People and reptiles

People affect the lives of reptiles – for good
and for bad. As the human population grows,
reptiles suffer and their lives are disturbed.
On the other hand, as we learn more
about reptiles, we can help
to protect them.

Everglades
National Park

Bush fires harm reptiles and their habitats

American
alligator

Tourism can destroy reptile habitats.
However, in national parks tourism is
strictly controlled. The Everglades National
Park, a wetland wilderness in Florida, USA,
protects 50 different kinds of reptile. Many
of them are rare or endangered.

releasing
Amazon turtle
hatchlings

Conservationists sometimes remove reptile eggs from their nests. They take the eggs to hatch out safely in a hatchery, away from predators and poachers. Later, the baby reptiles are returned to the wild.

Many roads run through snake habitats.

wood turtle

Transmitter sends a signal, showing where the turtle is.

Tracking devices help scientists follow the movements of endangered reptiles. When scientists find out more about an animal's way of life, they can work out better ways to protect it.

meeting a baby alligator in a zoo

Zoos and sanctuaries help reptiles by breeding them in captivity and then releasing them into the wild. They also help to educate visitors and turn them into wildlife supporters.

Evolution

The common ancestor to all **lizards** was living on Earth over 200 million years ago. It was very like the tuatara – a primitive, lizard-like creature that lives in New Zealand.

long-nosed leopard lizard

Snakes' distant ancestors probably had legs. Pythons have a pair of **claw-like spurs** on their body. Scientists believe they are the remains of legs.

• *python's spur*

Record breakers

The Galápagos tortoise is probably the oldest-living reptile. It lives for well over 100 years and has been known to reach the age of 176.

The saltwater crocodile is the world's largest reptile. It measures up to 7m and weighs about 1,000kg. It lives in rivers and along the coasts of India, Southeast Asia and Australia but can also swim far out to sea.

Plants

The saguaro cactus is a desert plant. Its stems and arms swell as its roots soak up water after a rare fall of rain.

Mangrove trees grow in calm water along tropical estuaries and coasts. Unlike most plants, they thrive in salt water. The mangroves' tangled roots prop them up in the sticky mud.

Habitats

• *Galápagos Islands*

The Galápagos Islands lie on the Equator. They are the rocky tips of volcanoes that erupted long ago. Though the climate is hot here all year round, the ocean waters are cold because of sea currents that flow up from Antarctica.

There are **five oceans** – the Pacific, the Atlantic, the Indian, the Arctic and the Southern. Together they cover about three-quarters of the Earth's surface.

More to explore

Reptiles evolved from amphibians like frogs and newts. Amphibians have thin, damp skins and lay their eggs in water. Reptiles developed watertight skins and eggs that did not dry out on land.

crocodile with nest on dry land

On a visit to the Galápagos Islands in 1835, the scientist Charles Darwin developed his **theory of evolution**. This said that living things adapt and develop over thousands of years to suit their surroundings. The best adapted species are more likely to survive.

finches in the Galápagos

The leatherback turtle is the fastest reptile and can swim at 35km/h. It swims in the open sea and travels as far as 6,000km between its feeding and breeding sites.

The fangs of the gaboon viper measure up to 5cm long – the longest of any snake. The fangs are hinged so they can fold back along the roof of the viper's mouth. They are shed every six to ten weeks and replaced by new fangs.

gaboon viper

coconuts

Coconut palms grow on tropical beaches. The fruits contain a seed, with food and water to sustain it, and are protected by a hard shell. Ripe fruit often washes out to sea. It floats to distant shores, where the seed shoots and grows.

Eucalyptus trees, or gum trees, grow in the Australian Outback. Forest fires are common in Australia but gum trees are adapted to survive. Buds under the bark start to grow when the fire has passed.

filled lizard in the desert

The heart of Australia is largely **desert** and has less than 250mm of rainfall a year. Hot deserts are harsh places, hot by day but cold at night. Desert animals and plants must survive on little water.

Tropical rainforests are thick forests that grow near the Equator. The weather is always warm and humid. The different layers of the forest are home to many animals and plants.

chameleon

Index